This journal belongs to:

_____

INSERT NAME

OTHER GUIDED JOURNALS & DIARIES
by
KINYATTA E. GRAY

I Miss You...

Daily Writing Prompts for Reflection, Remembrance, and Spirit Renewal

I Am A Man. I Have Feelings.

A Guided 90-Day Self-Reflections & Gratitude Journal for Men

Fashionista's Travel Diary

A Guided Travel Diary for Travel Planning & Reflections

The Queen's Manifestation Journal

Daily Writing Prompt for Manifesting the Life You Want

I'm Doing Me

The Ultimate Breakup Diary for Venting, Reflection & Spirit Renewal

Budget & Shop

A Monthly Personal Budget & Expense Tracker for Young Adults

While I'm Still Here

A Guided Expression Journal of Life, Love and Legacy for Those Preparing to Transition

My Life My Love My Truth

LGBTQ journal

My Crazy Teenage Life

The Ultimate Expression Diary for Venting, Self-Reflections and Self-Love

Sexy Baby Mama

Expectant & New Moms

Saved
With
Amazing
Grace

L♥VE

BEARS ALL THINGS, BELIEVES ALL THINGS, HOPES ALL THINGS, ENDURES ALL THINGS.

First Corinthians 13:7

wor

hip

Date: ___ / ___ / ___

Today's sermon was delivered by:

Today's sermon was about:

Today's scriptures I plan to study:

Today I Feel:

☐ Joyous
☐ Grateful
☐ Anointed
☐ In need of prayer
☐ Determined
☐ Like giving God all Praise

I gave this amount to the offering:

This worship song...

This testimony was powerful...

I need to keep _____ in prayer.

Upcoming Activities of Interest:

Volunteer Opportunities:

The next choir/dance/music ministry rehearsal is:

My spirit was renewed by:

I will practice what was taught today by:

SUNDAY WORSHIP NOTES & REFLECTIONS

Date: / /

Today's sermon was delivered by:	**Today I Feel:** ☐ Joyous ☐ Grateful ☐ Anointed ☐ In need of prayer ☐ Determined ☐ Like giving God all Praise
Today's sermon was about:	
Today's scriptures I plan to study:	

I gave this amount to the offering:

This worship song...

This testimony was powerful...

I need to keep   in prayer.

Upcoming Activities of Interest:

Volunteer Opportunities:

The next choir/dance/music ministry rehearsal is:

My spirit was renewed by:

I will practice what was taught today by:

SUNDAY WORSHIP NOTES & REFLECTIONS

Date: /   /

Today's sermon was delivered by:	**Today I Feel:** ☐ Joyous ☐ Grateful ☐ Anointed ☐ In need of prayer
Today's sermon was about:	☐ Determined ☐ Like giving God all Praise
Today's scriptures I plan to study:	

I gave this amount to the offering:

This worship song...

This testimony was powerful...

I need to keep _____ in prayer.

Upcoming Activities of Interest:

Volunteer Opportunities:

The next choir/dance/music ministry rehearsal is:

My spirit was renewed by:

I will practice what was taught today by:

Date: /   /

Today's sermon was delivered by:	**Today I Feel:**
	☐ Joyous
	☐ Grateful
Today's sermon was about:	☐ Anointed
	☐ In need of prayer
	☐ Determined
Today's scriptures I plan to study:	☐ Like giving God all Praise

I gave this amount to the offering:

This worship song...

This testimony was powerful...

I need to keep   in prayer.

Upcoming Activities of Interest:

Volunteer Opportunities:

The next choir/dance/music ministry rehearsal is:

My spirit was renewed by:

I will practice what was taught today by:

Date: ___ / ___ / ___

Today's sermon was delivered by:	**Today I Feel:**
	☐ Joyous
	☐ Grateful
Today's sermon was about:	☐ Anointed
	☐ In need of prayer
	☐ Determined
Today's scriptures I plan to study:	☐ Like giving God all Praise

I gave this amount to the offering:

This worship song...

This testimony was powerful...

I need to keep _____ in prayer.

Upcoming Activities of Interest:

Volunteer Opportunities:

The next choir/dance/music ministry rehearsal is:

My spirit was renewed by:

I will practice what was taught today by:

Date: /   /

	Today I Feel:
Today's sermon was delivered by:	☐ Joyous
	☐ Grateful
Today's sermon was about:	☐ Anointed
	☐ In need of prayer
	☐ Determined
Today's scriptures I plan to study:	☐ Like giving God all Praise

I gave this amount to the offering:

This worship song...

This testimony was powerful...

I need to keep _____ in prayer.

Upcoming Activities of Interest:

Volunteer Opportunities:

The next choir/dance/music ministry rehearsal is:

My spirit was renewed by:

I will practice what was taught today by:

SUNDAY WORSHIP NOTES & REFLECTIONS

Date: /   /

Today's sermon was delivered by:	**Today I Feel:**
	☐ Joyous
Today's sermon was about:	☐ Grateful
	☐ Anointed
	☐ In need of prayer
Today's scriptures I plan to study:	☐ Determined
	☐ Like giving God all Praise

I gave this amount to the offering:

This worship song...

This testimony was powerful...

I need to keep   in prayer.

Upcoming Activities of Interest:

Volunteer Opportunities:

The next choir/dance/music ministry rehearsal is:

My spirit was renewed by:

I will practice what was taught today by:

Date: /   /

Today's sermon was delivered by:	**Today I Feel:**
	☐ Joyous
	☐ Grateful
Today's sermon was about:	☐ Anointed
	☐ In need of prayer
	☐ Determined
Today's scriptures I plan to study:	☐ Like giving God all Praise

I gave this amount to the offering:

This worship song...

This testimony was powerful...

I need to keep _____ in prayer.

Upcoming Activities of Interest:

Volunteer Opportunities:

The next choir/dance/music ministry rehearsal is:

My spirit was renewed by:

I will practice what was taught today by:

SUNDAY WORSHIP NOTES & REFLECTIONS

Date: /   /

Today's sermon was delivered by:	**Today I Feel:**
	☐ Joyous
Today's sermon was about:	☐ Grateful
	☐ Anointed
	☐ In need of prayer
Today's scriptures I plan to study:	☐ Determined
	☐ Like giving God all Praise

I gave this amount to the offering:

This worship song...

This testimony was powerful...

I need to keep   in prayer.

Upcoming Activities of Interest:

Volunteer Opportunities:

The next choir/dance/music ministry rehearsal is:

My spirit was renewed by:

I will practice what was taught today by:

SUNDAY WORSHIP NOTES & REFLECTIONS

Date: /   /

	Today I Feel:
Today's sermon was delivered by:	☐ Joyous ☐ Grateful ☐ Anointed ☐ In need of prayer
Today's sermon was about:	☐ Determined ☐ Like giving God all Praise
Today's scriptures I plan to study:	

I gave this amount to the offering:

This worship song...

This testimony was powerful...

I need to keep   in prayer.

Upcoming Activities of Interest:

Volunteer Opportunities:

The next choir/dance/music ministry rehearsal is:

My spirit was renewed by:

I will practice what was taught today by:

SUNDAY WORSHIP NOTES & REFLECTIONS

Date: /   /

Today's sermon was delivered by:	**Today I Feel:** ☐ Joyous ☐ Grateful ☐ Anointed ☐ In need of prayer ☐ Determined ☐ Like giving God all Praise
Today's sermon was about:	
Today's scriptures I plan to study:	

I gave this amount to the offering:

This worship song...

This testimony was powerful...

I need to keep   in prayer.

Upcoming Activities of Interest:

Volunteer Opportunities:

The next choir/dance/music ministry rehearsal is:

My spirit was renewed by:

I will practice what was taught today by:

SUNDAY WORSHIP NOTES & REFLECTIONS

Date: /   /

Today's sermon was delivered by:	**Today I Feel:** ☐ Joyous ☐ Grateful ☐ Anointed ☐ In need of prayer ☐ Determined ☐ Like giving God all Praise
Today's sermon was about:	
Today's scriptures I plan to study:	

I gave this amount to the offering:

This worship song...

This testimony was powerful...

I need to keep   in prayer.

Upcoming Activities of Interest:

Volunteer Opportunities:

The next choir/dance/music ministry rehearsal is:

My spirit was renewed by:

I will practice what was taught today by:

Date: /   /

Today's sermon was delivered by:	**Today I Feel:**
	☐ Joyous
Today's sermon was about:	☐ Grateful
	☐ Anointed
	☐ In need of prayer
Today's scriptures I plan to study:	☐ Determined
	☐ Like giving God all Praise

I gave this amount to the offering:

This worship song...

This testimony was powerful...

I need to keep   in prayer.

Upcoming Activities of Interest:

Volunteer Opportunities:

The next choir/dance/music ministry rehearsal is:

My spirit was renewed by:

I will practice what was taught today by:

SUNDAY WORSHIP NOTES & REFLECTIONS

Date: /   /

Today's sermon was delivered by:	**Today I Feel:**
	☐ Joyous
	☐ Grateful
Today's sermon was about:	☐ Anointed
	☐ In need of prayer
Today's scriptures I plan to study:	☐ Determined
	☐ Like giving God all Praise

I gave this amount to the offering:

This worship song...

This testimony was powerful...

I need to keep _____ in prayer.

Upcoming Activities of Interest:

Volunteer Opportunities:

The next choir/dance/music ministry rehearsal is:

My spirit was renewed by:

I will practice what was taught today by:

Date: /   /

Today's sermon was delivered by:	**Today I Feel:** ☐ Joyous ☐ Grateful ☐ Anointed ☐ In need of prayer
Today's sermon was about:	☐ Determined ☐ Like giving God all Praise
Today's scriptures I plan to study:	

I gave this amount to the offering:

This worship song...

This testimony was powerful...

I need to keep   in prayer.

Upcoming Activities of Interest:

Volunteer Opportunities:

The next choir/dance/music ministry rehearsal is:

My spirit was renewed by:

I will practice what was taught today by:

Date: /   /

	Today I Feel:
Today's sermon was delivered by:	☐ Joyous
	☐ Grateful
Today's sermon was about:	☐ Anointed
	☐ In need of prayer
Today's scriptures I plan to study:	☐ Determined
	☐ Like giving God all Praise

I gave this amount to the offering:

This worship song...

This testimony was powerful...

I need to keep   in prayer.

Upcoming Activities of Interest:

Volunteer Opportunities:

The next choir/dance/music ministry rehearsal is:

My spirit was renewed by:

I will practice what was taught today by:

Date: /   /

Today's sermon was delivered by:	**Today I Feel:**
	☐ Joyous
	☐ Grateful
Today's sermon was about:	☐ Anointed
	☐ In need of prayer
	☐ Determined
Today's scriptures I plan to study:	☐ Like giving God all Praise

I gave this amount to the offering:

This worship song...

This testimony was powerful...

I need to keep   in prayer.

Upcoming Activities of Interest:

Volunteer Opportunities:

The next choir/dance/music ministry rehearsal is:

My spirit was renewed by:

I will practice what was taught today by:

SUNDAY WORSHIP NOTES & REFLECTIONS

Date: /   /

Today's sermon was delivered by:	**Today I Feel:** ☐ Joyous
Today's sermon was about:	☐ Grateful ☐ Anointed ☐ In need of prayer
Today's scriptures I plan to study:	☐ Determined ☐ Like giving God all Praise

I gave this amount to the offering:

This worship song...

This testimony was powerful...

I need to keep   in prayer.

Upcoming Activities of Interest:

Volunteer Opportunities:

The next choir/dance/music ministry rehearsal is:

My spirit was renewed by:

I will practice what was taught today by:

Date: /   /

Today's sermon was delivered by:

Today I Feel:
- ☐ Joyous
- ☐ Grateful
- ☐ Anointed
- ☐ In need of prayer
- ☐ Determined
- ☐ Like giving God all Praise

Today's sermon was about:

Today's scriptures I plan to study:

I gave this amount to the offering:

This worship song...

This testimony was powerful...

I need to keep   in prayer.

Upcoming Activities of Interest:

Volunteer Opportunities:

The next choir/dance/music ministry rehearsal is:

My spirit was renewed by:

I will practice what was taught today by:

Date: /   /

	Today I Feel:
Today's sermon was delivered by:	☐ Joyous
	☐ Grateful
Today's sermon was about:	☐ Anointed
	☐ In need of prayer
	☐ Determined
Today's scriptures I plan to study:	☐ Like giving God all Praise

I gave this amount to the offering:

This worship song...

This testimony was powerful...

I need to keep   in prayer.

Upcoming Activities of Interest:

Volunteer Opportunities:

The next choir/dance/music ministry rehearsal is:

My spirit was renewed by:

I will practice what was taught today by:

SUNDAY WORSHIP NOTES & REFLECTIONS

Date: /   /

Today's sermon was delivered by:	**Today I Feel:**
	☐ Joyous
Today's sermon was about:	☐ Grateful
	☐ Anointed
	☐ In need of prayer
Today's scriptures I plan to study:	☐ Determined
	☐ Like giving God all Praise

I gave this amount to the offering:

This worship song...

This testimony was powerful...

I need to keep   in prayer.

Upcoming Activities of Interest:

Volunteer Opportunities:

The next choir/dance/music ministry rehearsal is:

My spirit was renewed by:

I will practice what was taught today by:

Date: / /

Today's sermon was delivered by:	**Today I Feel:**
	☐ Joyous
	☐ Grateful
Today's sermon was about:	☐ Anointed
	☐ In need of prayer
	☐ Determined
Today's scriptures I plan to study:	☐ Like giving God all Praise

I gave this amount to the offering:

This worship song...

This testimony was powerful...

I need to keep _____ in prayer.

Upcoming Activities of Interest:

Volunteer Opportunities:

The next choir/dance/music ministry rehearsal is:

My spirit was renewed by:

I will practice what was taught today by:

Date: /   /

Today's sermon was delivered by:	**Today I Feel:**
	☐ Joyous
	☐ Grateful
Today's sermon was about:	☐ Anointed
	☐ In need of prayer
	☐ Determined
Today's scriptures I plan to study:	☐ Like giving God all Praise

I gave this amount to the offering:

This worship song...

This testimony was powerful...

I need to keep   in prayer.

Upcoming Activities of Interest:

Volunteer Opportunities:

The next choir/dance/music ministry rehearsal is:

My spirit was renewed by:

I will practice what was taught today by:

Date: /   /

	Today I Feel:
Today's sermon was delivered by:	☐ Joyous
	☐ Grateful
Today's sermon was about:	☐ Anointed
	☐ In need of prayer
	☐ Determined
Today's scriptures I plan to study:	☐ Like giving God all Praise

I gave this amount to the offering:

This worship song...

This testimony was powerful...

I need to keep _____ in prayer.

Upcoming Activities of Interest:

Volunteer Opportunities:

The next choir/dance/music ministry rehearsal is:

My spirit was renewed by:

I will practice what was taught today by:

SUNDAY WORSHIP NOTES & REFLECTIONS

Date: / /

Today's sermon was delivered by:	**Today I Feel:**
	☐ Joyous
	☐ Grateful
Today's sermon was about:	☐ Anointed
	☐ In need of prayer
	☐ Determined
Today's scriptures I plan to study:	☐ Like giving God all Praise

I gave this amount to the offering:

This worship song...

This testimony was powerful...

I need to keep   in prayer.

Upcoming Activities of Interest:

Volunteer Opportunities:

The next choir/dance/music ministry rehearsal is:

My spirit was renewed by:

I will practice what was taught today by:

SUNDAY WORSHIP NOTES & REFLECTIONS

Date: ___ / ___ / ___

Today's sermon was delivered by:	**Today I Feel:** ☐ Joyous ☐ Grateful ☐ Anointed ☐ In need of prayer
Today's sermon was about:	
Today's scriptures I plan to study:	☐ Determined ☐ Like giving God all Praise

I gave this amount to the offering:

This worship song...

This testimony was powerful...

I need to keep _____ in prayer.

Upcoming Activities of Interest:

Volunteer Opportunities:

The next choir/dance/music ministry rehearsal is:

My spirit was renewed by:

I will practice what was taught today by:

SUNDAY WORSHIP NOTES & REFLECTIONS

Date: /   /

Today's sermon was delivered by:	**Today I Feel:**
	☐ Joyous
	☐ Grateful
Today's sermon was about:	☐ Anointed
	☐ In need of prayer
	☐ Determined
Today's scriptures I plan to study:	☐ Like giving God all Praise

I gave this amount to the offering:

This worship song...

This testimony was powerful...

I need to keep   in prayer.

Upcoming Activities of Interest:

Volunteer Opportunities:

The next choir/dance/music ministry rehearsal is:

My spirit was renewed by:

I will practice what was taught today by:

SUNDAY WORSHIP NOTES & REFLECTIONS

Date: /   /

Today's sermon was delivered by:

Today I Feel:
- ☐ Joyous
- ☐ Grateful
- ☐ Anointed
- ☐ In need of prayer
- ☐ Determined
- ☐ Like giving God all Praise

Today's sermon was about:

Today's scriptures I plan to study:

I gave this amount to the offering:

This worship song...

This testimony was powerful...

I need to keep _____ in prayer.

Upcoming Activities of Interest:

Volunteer Opportunities:

The next choir/dance/music ministry rehearsal is:

My spirit was renewed by:

I will practice what was taught today by:

Date: /   /

Today's sermon was delivered by:	**Today I Feel:** ☐ Joyous ☐ Grateful ☐ Anointed ☐ In need of prayer ☐ Determined ☐ Like giving God all Praise
Today's sermon was about:	
Today's scriptures I plan to study:	

I gave this amount to the offering:

This worship song...

This testimony was powerful...

I need to keep   in prayer.

Upcoming Activities of Interest:

Volunteer Opportunities:

The next choir/dance/music ministry rehearsal is:

My spirit was renewed by:

I will practice what was taught today by:

Date: /   /

	Today I Feel:
Today's sermon was delivered by:	☐ Joyous
	☐ Grateful
Today's sermon was about:	☐ Anointed
	☐ In need of prayer
	☐ Determined
Today's scriptures I plan to study:	☐ Like giving God all Praise

I gave this amount to the offering:

This worship song...

This testimony was powerful...

I need to keep   in prayer.

Upcoming Activities of Interest:

Volunteer Opportunities:

The next choir/dance/music ministry rehearsal is:

My spirit was renewed by:

I will practice what was taught today by:

Date: /   /

Today's sermon was delivered by:	**Today I Feel:**
	☐ Joyous
Today's sermon was about:	☐ Grateful
	☐ Anointed
	☐ In need of prayer
Today's scriptures I plan to study:	☐ Determined
	☐ Like giving God all Praise

I gave this amount to the offering:

This worship song...

This testimony was powerful...

I need to keep   in prayer.

Upcoming Activities of Interest:

Volunteer Opportunities:

The next choir/dance/music ministry rehearsal is:

My spirit was renewed by:

I will practice what was taught today by:

Date: /   /

Today's sermon was delivered by:	**Today I Feel:**
	☐ Joyous
	☐ Grateful
Today's sermon was about:	☐ Anointed
	☐ In need of prayer
	☐ Determined
Today's scriptures I plan to study:	☐ Like giving God all Praise

I gave this amount to the offering:

This worship song...

This testimony was powerful...

I need to keep _____ in prayer.

Upcoming Activities of Interest:

Volunteer Opportunities:

The next choir/dance/music ministry rehearsal is:

My spirit was renewed by:

I will practice what was taught today by:

Date: /   /

Today's sermon was delivered by:	**Today I Feel:**
	☐ Joyous
	☐ Grateful
Today's sermon was about:	☐ Anointed
	☐ In need of prayer
	☐ Determined
Today's scriptures I plan to study:	☐ Like giving God all Praise

I gave this amount to the offering:

This worship song...

This testimony was powerful...

I need to keep   in prayer.

Upcoming Activities of Interest:

Volunteer Opportunities:

The next choir/dance/music ministry rehearsal is:

My spirit was renewed by:

I will practice what was taught today by:

SUNDAY WORSHIP NOTES & REFLECTIONS

Date: /   /

Today's sermon was delivered by:	**Today I Feel:**
	☐ Joyous
Today's sermon was about:	☐ Grateful
	☐ Anointed
	☐ In need of prayer
Today's scriptures I plan to study:	☐ Determined
	☐ Like giving God all Praise

I gave this amount to the offering:

This worship song...

This testimony was powerful...

I need to keep   in prayer.

Upcoming Activities of Interest:

Volunteer Opportunities:

The next choir/dance/music ministry rehearsal is:

My spirit was renewed by:

I will practice what was taught today by:

SUNDAY WORSHIP NOTES & REFLECTIONS

Date: /   /

Today's sermon was delivered by:	**Today I Feel:** ☐ Joyous ☐ Grateful ☐ Anointed ☐ In need of prayer ☐ Determined ☐ Like giving God all Praise
Today's sermon was about:	
Today's scriptures I plan to study:	

I gave this amount to the offering:

This worship song...

This testimony was powerful...

I need to keep   in prayer.

Upcoming Activities of Interest:

Volunteer Opportunities:

The next choir/dance/music ministry rehearsal is:

My spirit was renewed by:

I will practice what was taught today by:

Date: /   /

Today's sermon was delivered by:	**Today I Feel:**
	☐ Joyous
Today's sermon was about:	☐ Grateful
	☐ Anointed
	☐ In need of prayer
Today's scriptures I plan to study:	☐ Determined
	☐ Like giving God all Praise

I gave this amount to the offering:

This worship song...

This testimony was powerful...

I need to keep   in prayer.

Upcoming Activities of Interest:

Volunteer Opportunities:

The next choir/dance/music ministry rehearsal is:

My spirit was renewed by:

I will practice what was taught today by:

Date: /   /

Today's sermon was delivered by:	**Today I Feel:** ☐ Joyous
	☐ Grateful
Today's sermon was about:	☐ Anointed
	☐ In need of prayer
	☐ Determined
Today's scriptures I plan to study:	☐ Like giving God all Praise

I gave this amount to the offering:

This worship song...

This testimony was powerful...

I need to keep _____ in prayer.

Upcoming Activities of Interest:

Volunteer Opportunities:

The next choir/dance/music ministry rehearsal is:

My spirit was renewed by:

I will practice what was taught today by:

Date: ___ / ___ / ___

	Today I Feel:
Today's sermon was delivered by:	☐ Joyous
	☐ Grateful
Today's sermon was about:	☐ Anointed
	☐ In need of prayer
	☐ Determined
Today's scriptures I plan to study:	☐ Like giving God all Praise

I gave this amount to the offering:

This worship song...

This testimony was powerful...

I need to keep _____ in prayer.

Upcoming Activities of Interest:

Volunteer Opportunities:

The next choir/dance/music ministry rehearsal is:

My spirit was renewed by:

I will practice what was taught today by:

Date: /   /

Today's sermon was delivered by:	**Today I Feel:** ☐ Joyous ☐ Grateful
Today's sermon was about:	☐ Anointed ☐ In need of prayer
Today's scriptures I plan to study:	☐ Determined ☐ Like giving God all Praise

I gave this amount to the offering:

This worship song...

This testimony was powerful...

I need to keep   in prayer.

Upcoming Activities of Interest:

Volunteer Opportunities:

The next choir/dance/music ministry rehearsal is:

My spirit was renewed by:

I will practice what was taught today by:

SUNDAY WORSHIP NOTES & REFLECTIONS

Date: /   /

Today's sermon was delivered by:	**Today I Feel:** ☐ Joyous ☐ Grateful ☐ Anointed ☐ In need of prayer ☐ Determined ☐ Like giving God all Praise
Today's sermon was about:	
Today's scriptures I plan to study:	

I gave this amount to the offering:

This worship song...

This testimony was powerful...

I need to keep   in prayer.

Upcoming Activities of Interest:

Volunteer Opportunities:

The next choir/dance/music ministry rehearsal is:

My spirit was renewed by:

I will practice what was taught today by:

SUNDAY WORSHIP NOTES & REFLECTIONS

Date: /   /

Today's sermon was delivered by:	**Today I Feel:** ☐ Joyous
Today's sermon was about:	☐ Grateful ☐ Anointed ☐ In need of prayer
Today's scriptures I plan to study:	☐ Determined ☐ Like giving God all Praise

I gave this amount to the offering:

This worship song...

This testimony was powerful...

I need to keep   in prayer.

Upcoming Activities of Interest:

Volunteer Opportunities:

The next choir/dance/music ministry rehearsal is:

My spirit was renewed by:

I will practice what was taught today by:

Date: /   /

Today's sermon was delivered by:	**Today I Feel:** ☐ Joyous ☐ Grateful ☐ Anointed ☐ In need of prayer ☐ Determined ☐ Like giving God all Praise
Today's sermon was about:	
Today's scriptures I plan to study:	

I gave this amount to the offering:

This worship song...

This testimony was powerful...

I need to keep   in prayer.

Upcoming Activities of Interest:

Volunteer Opportunities:

The next choir/dance/music ministry rehearsal is:

My spirit was renewed by:

I will practice what was taught today by:

Date: /   /

	Today I Feel:
Today's sermon was delivered by:	☐ Joyous
	☐ Grateful
Today's sermon was about:	☐ Anointed
	☐ In need of prayer
Today's scriptures I plan to study:	☐ Determined
	☐ Like giving God all Praise

I gave this amount to the offering:

This worship song...

This testimony was powerful...

I need to keep   in prayer.

Upcoming Activities of Interest:

Volunteer Opportunities:

The next choir/dance/music ministry rehearsal is:

My spirit was renewed by:

I will practice what was taught today by:

Date: /   /

Today's sermon was delivered by:	**Today I Feel:**
	☐ Joyous
	☐ Grateful
Today's sermon was about:	☐ Anointed
	☐ In need of prayer
	☐ Determined
Today's scriptures I plan to study:	☐ Like giving God all Praise

I gave this amount to the offering:

This worship song...

This testimony was powerful...

I need to keep   in prayer.

Upcoming Activities of Interest:

Volunteer Opportunities:

The next choir/dance/music ministry rehearsal is:

My spirit was renewed by:

I will practice what was taught today by:

Date: / /

Today's sermon was delivered by:

Today's sermon was about:

Today's scriptures I plan to study:

Today I Feel:

☐ Joyous

☐ Grateful

☐ Anointed

☐ In need of prayer

☐ Determined

☐ Like giving God all Praise

I gave this amount to the offering:

This worship song...

This testimony was powerful...

I need to keep   in prayer.

Upcoming Activities of Interest:

Volunteer Opportunities:

The next choir/dance/music ministry rehearsal is:

My spirit was renewed by:

I will practice what was taught today by:

SUNDAY WORSHIP NOTES & REFLECTIONS

Date: / /

Today's sermon was delivered by:	**Today I Feel:** ☐ Joyous ☐ Grateful ☐ Anointed ☐ In need of prayer
Today's sermon was about:	
	☐ Determined ☐ Like giving God all Praise
Today's scriptures I plan to study:	

I gave this amount to the offering:

This worship song...

This testimony was powerful...

I need to keep _____ in prayer.

Upcoming Activities of Interest:

Volunteer Opportunities:

The next choir/dance/music ministry rehearsal is:

My spirit was renewed by:

I will practice what was taught today by:

Date: /   /

Today's sermon was delivered by:	**Today I Feel:**
	☐ Joyous
	☐ Grateful
Today's sermon was about:	☐ Anointed
	☐ In need of prayer
	☐ Determined
Today's scriptures I plan to study:	☐ Like giving God all Praise

I gave this amount to the offering:

This worship song...

This testimony was powerful...

I need to keep   in prayer.

Upcoming Activities of Interest:

Volunteer Opportunities:

The next choir/dance/music ministry rehearsal is:

My spirit was renewed by:

I will practice what was taught today by:

Date: /   /

Today's sermon was delivered by:	**Today I Feel:**
	☐ Joyous
Today's sermon was about:	☐ Grateful
	☐ Anointed
	☐ In need of prayer
Today's scriptures I plan to study:	☐ Determined
	☐ Like giving God all Praise

I gave this amount to the offering:

This worship song...

This testimony was powerful...

I need to keep   in prayer.

Upcoming Activities of Interest:

Volunteer Opportunities:

The next choir/dance/music ministry rehearsal is:

My spirit was renewed by:

I will practice what was taught today by:

SUNDAY WORSHIP NOTES & REFLECTIONS

Date: / /

	Today I Feel:
Today's sermon was delivered by:	☐ Joyous
	☐ Grateful
Today's sermon was about:	☐ Anointed
	☐ In need of prayer
	☐ Determined
Today's scriptures I plan to study:	☐ Like giving God all Praise

I gave this amount to the offering:

This worship song...

This testimony was powerful...

I need to keep   in prayer.

Upcoming Activities of Interest:

Volunteer Opportunities:

The next choir/dance/music ministry rehearsal is:

My spirit was renewed by:

I will practice what was taught today by:

Date: /   /

	Today I Feel:
Today's sermon was delivered by:	☐ Joyous
	☐ Grateful
Today's sermon was about:	☐ Anointed
	☐ In need of prayer
	☐ Determined
Today's scriptures I plan to study:	☐ Like giving God all Praise

I gave this amount to the offering:

This worship song...

This testimony was powerful...

I need to keep   in prayer.

Upcoming Activities of Interest:

Volunteer Opportunities:

The next choir/dance/music ministry rehearsal is:

My spirit was renewed by:

I will practice what was taught today by:

SUNDAY WORSHIP NOTES & REFLECTIONS

Date: /   /

Today's sermon was delivered by:	**Today I Feel:**
	☐ Joyous
Today's sermon was about:	☐ Grateful
	☐ Anointed
	☐ In need of prayer
Today's scriptures I plan to study:	☐ Determined
	☐ Like giving God all Praise

I gave this amount to the offering:

This worship song...

This testimony was powerful...

I need to keep   in prayer.

Upcoming Activities of Interest:

Volunteer Opportunities:

The next choir/dance/music ministry rehearsal is:

My spirit was renewed by:

I will practice what was taught today by:

SUNDAY WORSHIP NOTES & REFLECTIONS

Date: / /

	Today I Feel:
Today's sermon was delivered by:	☐ Joyous
	☐ Grateful
Today's sermon was about:	☐ Anointed
	☐ In need of prayer
Today's scriptures I plan to study:	☐ Determined
	☐ Like giving God all Praise

I gave this amount to the offering:

This worship song...

This testimony was powerful...

I need to keep in prayer.

Upcoming Activities of Interest:

Volunteer Opportunities:

The next choir/dance/music ministry rehearsal is:

My spirit was renewed by:

I will practice what was taught today by:

SUNDAY WORSHIP NOTES & REFLECTIONS

Date: /   /

Today's sermon was delivered by:	**Today I Feel:** ☐ Joyous
Today's sermon was about:	☐ Grateful ☐ Anointed ☐ In need of prayer
Today's scriptures I plan to study:	☐ Determined ☐ Like giving God all Praise

I gave this amount to the offering:

This worship song...

This testimony was powerful...

I need to keep   in prayer.

Upcoming Activities of Interest:

Volunteer Opportunities:

The next choir/dance/music ministry rehearsal is:

My spirit was renewed by:

I will practice what was taught today by:

Date: / /

Today's sermon was delivered by:	**Today I Feel:**
	☐ Joyous
Today's sermon was about:	☐ Grateful
	☐ Anointed
	☐ In need of prayer
Today's scriptures I plan to study:	☐ Determined
	☐ Like giving God all Praise

I gave this amount to the offering:

This worship song...

This testimony was powerful...

I need to keep _____ in prayer.

Upcoming Activities of Interest:

Volunteer Opportunities:

The next choir/dance/music ministry rehearsal is:

My spirit was renewed by:

I will practice what was taught today by:

SUNDAY WORSHIP NOTES & REFLECTIONS

Date: /   /

Today's sermon was delivered by:	**Today I Feel:**
	☐ Joyous
Today's sermon was about:	☐ Grateful
	☐ Anointed
	☐ In need of prayer
Today's scriptures I plan to study:	☐ Determined
	☐ Like giving God all Praise

I gave this amount to the offering:

This worship song...

This testimony was powerful...

I need to keep   in prayer.

Upcoming Activities of Interest:

Volunteer Opportunities:

The next choir/dance/music ministry rehearsal is:

My spirit was renewed by:

I will practice what was taught today by:

Date: ___ / ___ / ___

Today's sermon was delivered by:	**Today I Feel:** ☐ Joyous ☐ Grateful
Today's sermon was about:	☐ Anointed ☐ In need of prayer
Today's scriptures I plan to study:	☐ Determined ☐ Like giving God all Praise

I gave this amount to the offering:

This worship song...

This testimony was powerful...

I need to keep _____ in prayer.

Upcoming Activities of Interest:

Volunteer Opportunities:

The next choir/dance/music ministry rehearsal is:

My spirit was renewed by:

I will practice what was taught today by:

Date: /   /

Today's sermon was delivered by:	**Today I Feel:** ☐ Joyous ☐ Grateful ☐ Anointed ☐ In need of prayer
Today's sermon was about:	☐ Determined ☐ Like giving God all Praise
Today's scriptures I plan to study:	

I gave this amount to the offering:

This worship song...

This testimony was powerful...

I need to keep _____ in prayer.

Upcoming Activities of Interest:

Volunteer Opportunities:

The next choir/dance/music ministry rehearsal is:

My spirit was renewed by:

I will practice what was taught today by:

SUNDAY WORSHIP NOTES & REFLECTIONS

Date: / /

Today's sermon was delivered by:	**Today I Feel:**
	☐ Joyous
	☐ Grateful
Today's sermon was about:	☐ Anointed
	☐ In need of prayer
	☐ Determined
Today's scriptures I plan to study:	☐ Like giving God all Praise

I gave this amount to the offering:

This worship song...

This testimony was powerful...

I need to keep   in prayer.

Upcoming Activities of Interest:

Volunteer Opportunities:

The next choir/dance/music ministry rehearsal is:

My spirit was renewed by:

I will practice what was taught today by:

Date: /   /

Today's sermon was delivered by:

Today I Feel:

☐ Joyous
☐ Grateful
☐ Anointed
☐ In need of prayer

Today's sermon was about:

☐ Determined
☐ Like giving God all Praise

Today's scriptures I plan to study:

I gave this amount to the offering:

This worship song...

This testimony was powerful...

I need to keep   in prayer.

Upcoming Activities of Interest:

Volunteer Opportunities:

The next choir/dance/music ministry rehearsal is:

My spirit was renewed by:

I will practice what was taught today by:

SUNDAY WORSHIP NOTES & REFLECTIONS

Date: ___ / ___ / ___

Today's sermon was delivered by:	**Today I Feel:**
	☐ Joyous
Today's sermon was about:	☐ Grateful
	☐ Anointed
	☐ In need of prayer
Today's scriptures I plan to study:	☐ Determined
	☐ Like giving God all Praise

I gave this amount to the offering:

This worship song...

This testimony was powerful...

I need to keep _____ in prayer.

Upcoming Activities of Interest:

Volunteer Opportunities:

The next choir/dance/music ministry rehearsal is:

My spirit was renewed by:

I will practice what was taught today by:

Date: /   /

Today's sermon was delivered by:

Today's sermon was about:

Today's scriptures I plan to study:

Today I Feel:
- ☐ Joyous
- ☐ Grateful
- ☐ Anointed
- ☐ In need of prayer
- ☐ Determined
- ☐ Like giving God all Praise

I gave this amount to the offering:

This worship song...

This testimony was powerful...

I need to keep   in prayer.

Upcoming Activities of Interest:

Volunteer Opportunities:

The next choir/dance/music ministry rehearsal is:

My spirit was renewed by:

I will practice what was taught today by:

SUNDAY WORSHIP NOTES & REFLECTIONS

Date: ___ / ___ / ___

Today's sermon was delivered by:	**Today I Feel:**
	☐ Joyous
	☐ Grateful
Today's sermon was about:	☐ Anointed
	☐ In need of prayer
	☐ Determined
Today's scriptures I plan to study:	☐ Like giving God all Praise

I gave this amount to the offering:

This worship song...

This testimony was powerful...

I need to keep _____ in prayer.

Upcoming Activities of Interest:

Volunteer Opportunities:

The next choir/dance/music ministry rehearsal is:

My spirit was renewed by:

I will practice what was taught today by:

SUNDAY WORSHIP NOTES & REFLECTIONS

Date: /   /

Today's sermon was delivered by:	**Today I Feel:**
	☐ Joyous
	☐ Grateful
Today's sermon was about:	☐ Anointed
	☐ In need of prayer
	☐ Determined
Today's scriptures I plan to study:	☐ Like giving God all Praise

I gave this amount to the offering:

This worship song...

This testimony was powerful...

I need to keep   in prayer.

Upcoming Activities of Interest:

Volunteer Opportunities:

The next choir/dance/music ministry rehearsal is:

My spirit was renewed by:

I will practice what was taught today by:

Date: /   /

Today's sermon was delivered by:	**Today I Feel:**
	☐ Joyous
	☐ Grateful
Today's sermon was about:	☐ Anointed
	☐ In need of prayer
	☐ Determined
Today's scriptures I plan to study:	☐ Like giving God all Praise

I gave this amount to the offering:

This worship song...

This testimony was powerful...

I need to keep   in prayer.

Upcoming Activities of Interest:

Volunteer Opportunities:

The next choir/dance/music ministry rehearsal is:

My spirit was renewed by:

I will practice what was taught today by:

Date: /   /

	Today I Feel:
Today's sermon was delivered by:	☐ Joyous
	☐ Grateful
Today's sermon was about:	☐ Anointed
	☐ In need of prayer
Today's scriptures I plan to study:	☐ Determined
	☐ Like giving God all Praise

I gave this amount to the offering:

This worship song...

This testimony was powerful...

I need to keep   in prayer.

Upcoming Activities of Interest:

Volunteer Opportunities:

The next choir/dance/music ministry rehearsal is:

My spirit was renewed by:

I will practice what was taught today by:

Date: /   /

	Today I Feel:
Today's sermon was delivered by:	☐ Joyous
	☐ Grateful
Today's sermon was about:	☐ Anointed
	☐ In need of prayer
	☐ Determined
Today's scriptures I plan to study:	☐ Like giving God all Praise

I gave this amount to the offering:

This worship song...

This testimony was powerful...

I need to keep   in prayer.

Upcoming Activities of Interest:

Volunteer Opportunities:

The next choir/dance/music ministry rehearsal is:

My spirit was renewed by:

I will practice what was taught today by:

SUNDAY WORSHIP NOTES & REFLECTIONS

Date: /   /

Today's sermon was delivered by:	**Today I Feel:**
	☐ Joyous
Today's sermon was about:	☐ Grateful
	☐ Anointed
	☐ In need of prayer
Today's scriptures I plan to study:	☐ Determined
	☐ Like giving God all Praise

I gave this amount to the offering:

This worship song...

This testimony was powerful...

I need to keep   in prayer.

Upcoming Activities of Interest:

Volunteer Opportunities:

The next choir/dance/music ministry rehearsal is:

My spirit was renewed by:

I will practice what was taught today by:

Date: /   /

Today's sermon was delivered by:	**Today I Feel:**
	☐ Joyous
	☐ Grateful
Today's sermon was about:	☐ Anointed
	☐ In need of prayer
	☐ Determined
Today's scriptures I plan to study:	☐ Like giving God all Praise

I gave this amount to the offering:

This worship song...

This testimony was powerful...

I need to keep   in prayer.

Upcoming Activities of Interest:

Volunteer Opportunities:

The next choir/dance/music ministry rehearsal is:

My spirit was renewed by:

I will practice what was taught today by:

SUNDAY WORSHIP NOTES & REFLECTIONS

Date: /   /

Today's sermon was delivered by:	**Today I Feel:** ☐ Joyous ☐ Grateful ☐ Anointed ☐ In need of prayer ☐ Determined ☐ Like giving God all Praise
Today's sermon was about:	
Today's scriptures I plan to study:	

I gave this amount to the offering:

This worship song...

This testimony was powerful...

I need to keep   in prayer.

Upcoming Activities of Interest:

Volunteer Opportunities:

The next choir/dance/music ministry rehearsal is:

My spirit was renewed by:

I will practice what was taught today by:

SUNDAY WORSHIP NOTES & REFLECTIONS

Date: /   /

Today's sermon was delivered by:	**Today I Feel:**
	☐ Joyous
Today's sermon was about:	☐ Grateful
	☐ Anointed
	☐ In need of prayer
Today's scriptures I plan to study:	☐ Determined
	☐ Like giving God all Praise

I gave this amount to the offering:

This worship song...

This testimony was powerful...

I need to keep   in prayer.

Upcoming Activities of Interest:

Volunteer Opportunities:

The next choir/dance/music ministry rehearsal is:

My spirit was renewed by:

I will practice what was taught today by:

SUNDAY WORSHIP NOTES & REFLECTIONS

Date: /   /

Today's sermon was delivered by:	**Today I Feel:**
	☐ Joyous
Today's sermon was about:	☐ Grateful
	☐ Anointed
	☐ In need of prayer
Today's scriptures I plan to study:	☐ Determined
	☐ Like giving God all Praise

I gave this amount to the offering:

This worship song...

This testimony was powerful...

I need to keep _____ in prayer.

Upcoming Activities of Interest:

Volunteer Opportunities:

The next choir/dance/music ministry rehearsal is:

My spirit was renewed by:

I will practice what was taught today by:

Date: /   /

Today's sermon was delivered by:	**Today I Feel:** ☐ Joyous ☐ Grateful ☐ Anointed ☐ In need of prayer ☐ Determined ☐ Like giving God all Praise
Today's sermon was about:	
Today's scriptures I plan to study:	

I gave this amount to the offering:

This worship song...

This testimony was powerful...

I need to keep   in prayer.

Upcoming Activities of Interest:

Volunteer Opportunities:

The next choir/dance/music ministry rehearsal is:

My spirit was renewed by:

I will practice what was taught today by:

SUNDAY WORSHIP NOTES & REFLECTIONS

Date: /   /

Today's sermon was delivered by:	Today I Feel:
	☐ Joyous
	☐ Grateful
Today's sermon was about:	☐ Anointed
	☐ In need of prayer
	☐ Determined
Today's scriptures I plan to study:	☐ Like giving God all Praise

I gave this amount to the offering:

This worship song...

This testimony was powerful...

I need to keep   in prayer.

Upcoming Activities of Interest:

Volunteer Opportunities:

The next choir/dance/music ministry rehearsal is:

My spirit was renewed by:

I will practice what was taught today by:

Date: /   /

Today's sermon was delivered by:	**Today I Feel:**
	☐ Joyous
	☐ Grateful
Today's sermon was about:	☐ Anointed
	☐ In need of prayer
	☐ Determined
Today's scriptures I plan to study:	☐ Like giving God all Praise

I gave this amount to the offering:

This worship song...

This testimony was powerful...

I need to keep   in prayer.

Upcoming Activities of Interest:

Volunteer Opportunities:

The next choir/dance/music ministry rehearsal is:

My spirit was renewed by:

I will practice what was taught today by:

Date: /   /

Today's sermon was delivered by:	**Today I Feel:** ☐ Joyous ☐ Grateful ☐ Anointed ☐ In need of prayer
Today's sermon was about:	☐ Determined ☐ Like giving God all Praise
Today's scriptures I plan to study:	

I gave this amount to the offering:

This worship song...

This testimony was powerful...

I need to keep   in prayer.

Upcoming Activities of Interest:

Volunteer Opportunities:

The next choir/dance/music ministry rehearsal is:

My spirit was renewed by:

I will practice what was taught today by:

Date: /   /

Today's sermon was delivered by:	**Today I Feel:** ☐ Joyous ☐ Grateful ☐ Anointed ☐ In need of prayer ☐ Determined ☐ Like giving God all Praise
Today's sermon was about:	
Today's scriptures I plan to study:	

I gave this amount to the offering:

This worship song...

This testimony was powerful...

I need to keep   in prayer.

Upcoming Activities of Interest:

Volunteer Opportunities:

The next choir/dance/music ministry rehearsal is:

My spirit was renewed by:

I will practice what was taught today by:

Date: /   /

Today's sermon was delivered by:	**Today I Feel:**
	☐ Joyous
Today's sermon was about:	☐ Grateful
	☐ Anointed
	☐ In need of prayer
Today's scriptures I plan to study:	☐ Determined
	☐ Like giving God all Praise

I gave this amount to the offering:

This worship song...

This testimony was powerful...

I need to keep   in prayer.

Upcoming Activities of Interest:

Volunteer Opportunities:

The next choir/dance/music ministry rehearsal is:

My spirit was renewed by:

I will practice what was taught today by:

SUNDAY WORSHIP NOTES & REFLECTIONS

Date: /   /

Today's sermon was delivered by:	**Today I Feel:**
	☐ Joyous
Today's sermon was about:	☐ Grateful
	☐ Anointed
	☐ In need of prayer
Today's scriptures I plan to study:	☐ Determined
	☐ Like giving God all Praise

I gave this amount to the offering:

This worship song...

This testimony was powerful...

I need to keep _____ in prayer.

Upcoming Activities of Interest:

Volunteer Opportunities:

The next choir/dance/music ministry rehearsal is:

My spirit was renewed by:

I will practice what was taught today by:

SUNDAY WORSHIP NOTES & REFLECTIONS

Date: / /

Today's sermon was delivered by:	**Today I Feel:** ☐ Joyous
Today's sermon was about:	☐ Grateful ☐ Anointed ☐ In need of prayer
Today's scriptures I plan to study:	☐ Determined ☐ Like giving God all Praise

I gave this amount to the offering:

This worship song...

This testimony was powerful...

I need to keep   in prayer.

Upcoming Activities of Interest:

Volunteer Opportunities:

The next choir/dance/music ministry rehearsal is:

My spirit was renewed by:

I will practice what was taught today by:

SUNDAY WORSHIP NOTES & REFLECTIONS

Date: / /

Today's sermon was delivered by:	**Today I Feel:** ☐ Joyous ☐ Grateful ☐ Anointed ☐ In need of prayer ☐ Determined ☐ Like giving God all Praise
Today's sermon was about:	
Today's scriptures I plan to study:	

I gave this amount to the offering:

This worship song...

This testimony was powerful...

I need to keep   in prayer.

Upcoming Activities of Interest:

Volunteer Opportunities:

The next choir/dance/music ministry rehearsal is:

My spirit was renewed by:

I will practice what was taught today by:

Date: /   /

Today's sermon was delivered by:	**Today I Feel:** ☐ Joyous ☐ Grateful ☐ Anointed ☐ In need of prayer
Today's sermon was about:	
Today's scriptures I plan to study:	☐ Determined ☐ Like giving God all Praise

I gave this amount to the offering:

This worship song...

This testimony was powerful...

I need to keep   in prayer.

Upcoming Activities of Interest:

Volunteer Opportunities:

The next choir/dance/music ministry rehearsal is:

My spirit was renewed by:

I will practice what was taught today by:

SUNDAY WORSHIP NOTES & REFLECTIONS

Date: /   /

Today's sermon was delivered by:	**Today I Feel:**
	☐ Joyous
	☐ Grateful
Today's sermon was about:	☐ Anointed
	☐ In need of prayer
	☐ Determined
Today's scriptures I plan to study:	☐ Like giving God all Praise

I gave this amount to the offering:

This worship song...

This testimony was powerful...

I need to keep _____ in prayer.

Upcoming Activities of Interest:

Volunteer Opportunities:

The next choir/dance/music ministry rehearsal is:

My spirit was renewed by:

I will practice what was taught today by:

SUNDAY WORSHIP NOTES & REFLECTIONS

Date: /   /

Today's sermon was delivered by:	**Today I Feel:**
	☐ Joyous
Today's sermon was about:	☐ Grateful
	☐ Anointed
	☐ In need of prayer
Today's scriptures I plan to study:	☐ Determined
	☐ Like giving God all Praise

I gave this amount to the offering:

This worship song...

This testimony was powerful...

I need to keep   in prayer.

Upcoming Activities of Interest:

Volunteer Opportunities:

The next choir/dance/music ministry rehearsal is:

My spirit was renewed by:

I will practice what was taught today by:

Date: /   /

Today's sermon was delivered by:	**Today I Feel:**
	☐ Joyous
	☐ Grateful
Today's sermon was about:	☐ Anointed
	☐ In need of prayer
	☐ Determined
Today's scriptures I plan to study:	☐ Like giving God all Praise

I gave this amount to the offering:

This worship song...

This testimony was powerful...

I need to keep   in prayer.

Upcoming Activities of Interest:

Volunteer Opportunities:

The next choir/dance/music ministry rehearsal is:

My spirit was renewed by:

I will practice what was taught today by:

Date: ___ / ___ / ___

Today's sermon was delivered by:	**Today I Feel:** ☐ Joyous ☐ Grateful ☐ Anointed ☐ In need of prayer ☐ Determined ☐ Like giving God all Praise
Today's sermon was about:	
Today's scriptures I plan to study:	

I gave this amount to the offering:

This worship song...

This testimony was powerful...

I need to keep _____ in prayer.

Upcoming Activities of Interest:

Volunteer Opportunities:

The next choir/dance/music ministry rehearsal is:

My spirit was renewed by:

I will practice what was taught today by:

Date: /   /

Today's sermon was delivered by:	**Today I Feel:** ☐ Joyous ☐ Grateful ☐ Anointed
Today's sermon was about:	☐ In need of prayer ☐ Determined
Today's scriptures I plan to study:	☐ Like giving God all Praise

I gave this amount to the offering:

This worship song...

This testimony was powerful...

I need to keep   in prayer.

Upcoming Activities of Interest:

Volunteer Opportunities:

The next choir/dance/music ministry rehearsal is:

My spirit was renewed by:

I will practice what was taught today by:

SUNDAY WORSHIP NOTES & REFLECTIONS

Date: /   /

Today's sermon was delivered by:	**Today I Feel:**
	☐ Joyous
	☐ Grateful
Today's sermon was about:	☐ Anointed
	☐ In need of prayer
	☐ Determined
Today's scriptures I plan to study:	☐ Like giving God all Praise

I gave this amount to the offering:

This worship song...

This testimony was powerful...

I need to keep   in prayer.

Upcoming Activities of Interest:

Volunteer Opportunities:

The next choir/dance/music ministry rehearsal is:

My spirit was renewed by:

I will practice what was taught today by:

SUNDAY WORSHIP NOTES & REFLECTIONS

Date: / /

	Today I Feel:
Today's sermon was delivered by:	☐ Joyous
	☐ Grateful
Today's sermon was about:	☐ Anointed
	☐ In need of prayer
Today's scriptures I plan to study:	☐ Determined
	☐ Like giving God all Praise

I gave this amount to the offering:

This worship song...

This testimony was powerful...

I need to keep   in prayer.

Upcoming Activities of Interest:

Volunteer Opportunities:

The next choir/dance/music ministry rehearsal is:

My spirit was renewed by:

I will practice what was taught today by:

SUNDAY WORSHIP NOTES & REFLECTIONS

Date: /   /

Today's sermon was delivered by:	**Today I Feel:** ☐ Joyous ☐ Grateful ☐ Anointed ☐ In need of prayer
Today's sermon was about:	☐ Determined ☐ Like giving God all Praise
Today's scriptures I plan to study:	

I gave this amount to the offering:

This worship song...

This testimony was powerful...

I need to keep _____ in prayer.

Upcoming Activities of Interest:

Volunteer Opportunities:

The next choir/dance/music ministry rehearsal is:

My spirit was renewed by:

I will practice what was taught today by:

Date: ___ / ___ / ___

Today's sermon was delivered by:	**Today I Feel:**
	☐ Joyous
	☐ Grateful
Today's sermon was about:	☐ Anointed
	☐ In need of prayer
	☐ Determined
Today's scriptures I plan to study:	☐ Like giving God all Praise

I gave this amount to the offering:

This worship song...

This testimony was powerful...

I need to keep _____ in prayer.

Upcoming Activities of Interest:

Volunteer Opportunities:

The next choir/dance/music ministry rehearsal is:

My spirit was renewed by:

I will practice what was taught today by:

Date: /   /

Today's sermon was delivered by:	**Today I Feel:** ☐ Joyous ☐ Grateful ☐ Anointed ☐ In need of prayer ☐ Determined ☐ Like giving God all Praise
Today's sermon was about:	
Today's scriptures I plan to study:	

I gave this amount to the offering:

This worship song...

This testimony was powerful...

I need to keep   in prayer.

Upcoming Activities of Interest:

Volunteer Opportunities:

The next choir/dance/music ministry rehearsal is:

My spirit was renewed by:

I will practice what was taught today by:

SUNDAY WORSHIP NOTES & REFLECTIONS

Date: ___ / ___ / ___

Today's sermon was delivered by:	**Today I Feel:** ☐ Joyous ☐ Grateful ☐ Anointed ☐ In need of prayer ☐ Determined ☐ Like giving God all Praise
Today's sermon was about:	
Today's scriptures I plan to study:	

I gave this amount to the offering:

This worship song...

This testimony was powerful...

I need to keep _____ in prayer.

Upcoming Activities of Interest:

Volunteer Opportunities:

The next choir/dance/music ministry rehearsal is:

My spirit was renewed by:

I will practice what was taught today by:

Date: /   /

	Today I Feel:
Today's sermon was delivered by:	☐ Joyous
	☐ Grateful
Today's sermon was about:	☐ Anointed
	☐ In need of prayer
	☐ Determined
Today's scriptures I plan to study:	☐ Like giving God all Praise

I gave this amount to the offering:

This worship song...

This testimony was powerful...

I need to keep   in prayer.

Upcoming Activities of Interest:

Volunteer Opportunities:

The next choir/dance/music ministry rehearsal is:

My spirit was renewed by:

I will practice what was taught today by:

Date: /   /

Today's sermon was delivered by:	**Today I Feel:**
	☐ Joyous
	☐ Grateful
Today's sermon was about:	☐ Anointed
	☐ In need of prayer
	☐ Determined
Today's scriptures I plan to study:	☐ Like giving God all Praise

I gave this amount to the offering:

This worship song...

This testimony was powerful...

I need to keep   in prayer.

Upcoming Activities of Interest:

Volunteer Opportunities:

The next choir/dance/music ministry rehearsal is:

My spirit was renewed by:

I will practice what was taught today by:

Date: /   /

Today's sermon was delivered by:	**Today I Feel:**
	☐ Joyous
Today's sermon was about:	☐ Grateful
	☐ Anointed
	☐ In need of prayer
Today's scriptures I plan to study:	☐ Determined
	☐ Like giving God all Praise

I gave this amount to the offering:

This worship song...

This testimony was powerful...

I need to keep   in prayer.

Upcoming Activities of Interest:

Volunteer Opportunities:

The next choir/dance/music ministry rehearsal is:

My spirit was renewed by:

I will practice what was taught today by:

Date: /   /

Today's sermon was delivered by:	**Today I Feel:**
	☐ Joyous
Today's sermon was about:	☐ Grateful
	☐ Anointed
	☐ In need of prayer
Today's scriptures I plan to study:	☐ Determined
	☐ Like giving God all Praise

I gave this amount to the offering:

This worship song...

This testimony was powerful...

I need to keep   in prayer.

Upcoming Activities of Interest:

Volunteer Opportunities:

The next choir/dance/music ministry rehearsal is:

My spirit was renewed by:

I will practice what was taught today by:

SUNDAY WORSHIP NOTES & REFLECTIONS

Date: /   /

Today's sermon was delivered by:	**Today I Feel:** ☐ Joyous ☐ Grateful ☐ Anointed ☐ In need of prayer ☐ Determined ☐ Like giving God all Praise
Today's sermon was about:	
Today's scriptures I plan to study:	

I gave this amount to the offering:

This worship song...

This testimony was powerful...

I need to keep   in prayer.

Upcoming Activities of Interest:

Volunteer Opportunities:

The next choir/dance/music ministry rehearsal is:

My spirit was renewed by:

I will practice what was taught today by:

SUNDAY WORSHIP NOTES & REFLECTIONS

Date: /   /

Today's sermon was delivered by:	**Today I Feel:**
	☐ Joyous
	☐ Grateful
Today's sermon was about:	☐ Anointed
	☐ In need of prayer
	☐ Determined
Today's scriptures I plan to study:	☐ Like giving God all Praise

I gave this amount to the offering:

This worship song...

This testimony was powerful...

I need to keep   in prayer.

Upcoming Activities of Interest:

Volunteer Opportunities:

The next choir/dance/music ministry rehearsal is:

My spirit was renewed by:

I will practice what was taught today by:

SUNDAY WORSHIP NOTES & REFLECTIONS

Date: /   /

Today's sermon was delivered by:	**Today I Feel:**
	☐ Joyous
Today's sermon was about:	☐ Grateful
	☐ Anointed
	☐ In need of prayer
Today's scriptures I plan to study:	☐ Determined
	☐ Like giving God all Praise

I gave this amount to the offering:

This worship song...

This testimony was powerful...

I need to keep   in prayer.

Upcoming Activities of Interest:

Volunteer Opportunities:

The next choir/dance/music ministry rehearsal is:

My spirit was renewed by:

I will practice what was taught today by:

SUNDAY WORSHIP NOTES & REFLECTIONS

Date: /   /

Today's sermon was delivered by:	**Today I Feel:**
	☐ Joyous
	☐ Grateful
Today's sermon was about:	☐ Anointed
	☐ In need of prayer
	☐ Determined
Today's scriptures I plan to study:	☐ Like giving God all Praise

I gave this amount to the offering:

This worship song...

This testimony was powerful...

I need to keep   in prayer.

Upcoming Activities of Interest:

Volunteer Opportunities:

The next choir/dance/music ministry rehearsal is:

My spirit was renewed by:

I will practice what was taught today by:

SUNDAY WORSHIP NOTES & REFLECTIONS

Date: /   /

Today's sermon was delivered by:	**Today I Feel:** ☐ Joyous ☐ Grateful ☐ Anointed ☐ In need of prayer ☐ Determined ☐ Like giving God all Praise
Today's sermon was about:	
Today's scriptures I plan to study:	

I gave this amount to the offering:

This worship song...

This testimony was powerful...

I need to keep   in prayer.

Upcoming Activities of Interest:

Volunteer Opportunities:

The next choir/dance/music ministry rehearsal is:

My spirit was renewed by:

I will practice what was taught today by:

Date: /   /

	Today I Feel:
Today's sermon was delivered by:	☐ Joyous
	☐ Grateful
Today's sermon was about:	☐ Anointed
	☐ In need of prayer
	☐ Determined
Today's scriptures I plan to study:	☐ Like giving God all Praise

I gave this amount to the offering:

This worship song...

This testimony was powerful...

I need to keep   in prayer.

Upcoming Activities of Interest:

Volunteer Opportunities:

The next choir/dance/music ministry rehearsal is:

My spirit was renewed by:

I will practice what was taught today by:

Date: /   /

Today's sermon was delivered by:	**Today I Feel:**
	☐ Joyous
Today's sermon was about:	☐ Grateful
	☐ Anointed
	☐ In need of prayer
Today's scriptures I plan to study:	☐ Determined
	☐ Like giving God all Praise

I gave this amount to the offering:

This worship song...

This testimony was powerful...

I need to keep   in prayer.

Upcoming Activities of Interest:

Volunteer Opportunities:

The next choir/dance/music ministry rehearsal is:

My spirit was renewed by:

I will practice what was taught today by:

Date: /   /

Today's sermon was delivered by:	**Today I Feel:**
	☐ Joyous
	☐ Grateful
Today's sermon was about:	☐ Anointed
	☐ In need of prayer
	☐ Determined
Today's scriptures I plan to study:	☐ Like giving God all Praise

I gave this amount to the offering:

This worship song...

This testimony was powerful...

I need to keep   in prayer.

Upcoming Activities of Interest:

Volunteer Opportunities:

The next choir/dance/music ministry rehearsal is:

My spirit was renewed by:

I will practice what was taught today by:

Date: /   /

Today's sermon was delivered by:	**Today I Feel:**
	☐ Joyous
Today's sermon was about:	☐ Grateful
	☐ Anointed
	☐ In need of prayer
Today's scriptures I plan to study:	☐ Determined
	☐ Like giving God all Praise

I gave this amount to the offering:

This worship song...

This testimony was powerful...

I need to keep   in prayer.

Upcoming Activities of Interest:

Volunteer Opportunities:

The next choir/dance/music ministry rehearsal is:

My spirit was renewed by:

I will practice what was taught today by:

SUNDAY WORSHIP NOTES & REFLECTIONS

Date: /   /

Today's sermon was delivered by:	**Today I Feel:**
	☐ Joyous
	☐ Grateful
Today's sermon was about:	☐ Anointed
	☐ In need of prayer
	☐ Determined
Today's scriptures I plan to study:	☐ Like giving God all Praise

I gave this amount to the offering:

This worship song...

This testimony was powerful...

I need to keep   in prayer.

Upcoming Activities of Interest:

Volunteer Opportunities:

The next choir/dance/music ministry rehearsal is:

My spirit was renewed by:

I will practice what was taught today by:

Date: /   /

Today's sermon was delivered by:	**Today I Feel:**
	☐ Joyous
Today's sermon was about:	☐ Grateful
	☐ Anointed
	☐ In need of prayer
Today's scriptures I plan to study:	☐ Determined
	☐ Like giving God all Praise

I gave this amount to the offering:

This worship song...

This testimony was powerful...

I need to keep   in prayer.

Upcoming Activities of Interest:

Volunteer Opportunities:

The next choir/dance/music ministry rehearsal is:

My spirit was renewed by:

I will practice what was taught today by:

Date: /   /

	Today I Feel:
Today's sermon was delivered by:	☐ Joyous
	☐ Grateful
Today's sermon was about:	☐ Anointed
	☐ In need of prayer
Today's scriptures I plan to study:	☐ Determined
	☐ Like giving God all Praise

I gave this amount to the offering:

This worship song...

This testimony was powerful...

I need to keep   in prayer.

Upcoming Activities of Interest:

Volunteer Opportunities:

The next choir/dance/music ministry rehearsal is:

My spirit was renewed by:

I will practice what was taught today by:

Date: /   /

Today's sermon was delivered by:	**Today I Feel:** ☐ Joyous ☐ Grateful ☐ Anointed ☐ In need of prayer ☐ Determined ☐ Like giving God all Praise
Today's sermon was about:	
Today's scriptures I plan to study:	

I gave this amount to the offering:

This worship song...

This testimony was powerful...

I need to keep   in prayer.

Upcoming Activities of Interest:

Volunteer Opportunities:

The next choir/dance/music ministry rehearsal is:

My spirit was renewed by:

I will practice what was taught today by:

SUNDAY WORSHIP NOTES & REFLECTIONS

Date: /   /

Today's sermon was delivered by:	**Today I Feel:**
	☐ Joyous
	☐ Grateful
Today's sermon was about:	☐ Anointed
	☐ In need of prayer
	☐ Determined
Today's scriptures I plan to study:	☐ Like giving God all Praise

I gave this amount to the offering:

This worship song...

This testimony was powerful...

I need to keep _____ in prayer.

Upcoming Activities of Interest:

Volunteer Opportunities:

The next choir/dance/music ministry rehearsal is:

My spirit was renewed by:

I will practice what was taught today by:

SUNDAY WORSHIP NOTES & REFLECTIONS

Date: _____ / _____ / _____

Today's sermon was delivered by:	**Today I Feel:** ☐ Joyous ☐ Grateful ☐ Anointed ☐ In need of prayer ☐ Determined ☐ Like giving God all Praise
Today's sermon was about:	
Today's scriptures I plan to study:	

I gave this amount to the offering:

This worship song...

This testimony was powerful...

I need to keep _____ in prayer.

Upcoming Activities of Interest:

Volunteer Opportunities:

The next choir/dance/music ministry rehearsal is:

My spirit was renewed by:

I will practice what was taught today by:

Date: /   /

	Today I Feel:
Today's sermon was delivered by:	☐ Joyous
	☐ Grateful
Today's sermon was about:	☐ Anointed
	☐ In need of prayer
Today's scriptures I plan to study:	☐ Determined
	☐ Like giving God all Praise

I gave this amount to the offering:

This worship song...

This testimony was powerful...

I need to keep   in prayer.

Upcoming Activities of Interest:

Volunteer Opportunities:

The next choir/dance/music ministry rehearsal is:

My spirit was renewed by:

I will practice what was taught today by:

Date: /   /

Today's sermon was delivered by:

Today I Feel:

☐ Joyous

☐ Grateful

Today's sermon was about:

☐ Anointed

☐ In need of prayer

☐ Determined

Today's scriptures I plan to study:

☐ Like giving God all Praise

I gave this amount to the offering:

This worship song...

This testimony was powerful...

I need to keep   in prayer.

Upcoming Activities of Interest:

Volunteer Opportunities:

The next choir/dance/music ministry rehearsal is:

My spirit was renewed by:

I will practice what was taught today by:

SUNDAY WORSHIP NOTES & REFLECTIONS

Date: /   /

Today's sermon was delivered by:	**Today I Feel:**
	☐ Joyous
	☐ Grateful
Today's sermon was about:	☐ Anointed
	☐ In need of prayer
	☐ Determined
Today's scriptures I plan to study:	☐ Like giving God all Praise

I gave this amount to the offering:

This worship song...

This testimony was powerful...

I need to keep   in prayer.

Upcoming Activities of Interest:

Volunteer Opportunities:

The next choir/dance/music ministry rehearsal is:

My spirit was renewed by:

I will practice what was taught today by:

Date: /   /

Today's sermon was delivered by:	**Today I Feel:**
	☐ Joyous
Today's sermon was about:	☐ Grateful
	☐ Anointed
	☐ In need of prayer
Today's scriptures I plan to study:	☐ Determined
	☐ Like giving God all Praise

I gave this amount to the offering:

This worship song...

This testimony was powerful...

I need to keep   in prayer.

Upcoming Activities of Interest:

Volunteer Opportunities:

The next choir/dance/music ministry rehearsal is:

My spirit was renewed by:

I will practice what was taught today by:

Date: /   /

Today's sermon was delivered by:	**Today I Feel:**
	☐ Joyous
	☐ Grateful
Today's sermon was about:	☐ Anointed
	☐ In need of prayer
	☐ Determined
Today's scriptures I plan to study:	☐ Like giving God all Praise

I gave this amount to the offering:

This worship song...

This testimony was powerful...

I need to keep   in prayer.

Upcoming Activities of Interest:

Volunteer Opportunities:

The next choir/dance/music ministry rehearsal is:

My spirit was renewed by:

I will practice what was taught today by:

Date: /   /

Today's sermon was delivered by:

Today I Feel:
- ☐ Joyous
- ☐ Grateful

Today's sermon was about:
- ☐ Anointed
- ☐ In need of prayer
- ☐ Determined

Today's scriptures I plan to study:
- ☐ Like giving God all Praise

I gave this amount to the offering:

This worship song...

This testimony was powerful...

I need to keep   in prayer.

Upcoming Activities of Interest:

Volunteer Opportunities:

The next choir/dance/music ministry rehearsal is:

My spirit was renewed by:

I will practice what was taught today by:

Date: /   /

Today's sermon was delivered by:	**Today I Feel:** ☐ Joyous ☐ Grateful ☐ Anointed ☐ In need of prayer
Today's sermon was about:	☐ Determined ☐ Like giving God all Praise
Today's scriptures I plan to study:	

I gave this amount to the offering:

This worship song...

This testimony was powerful...

I need to keep   in prayer.

Upcoming Activities of Interest:

Volunteer Opportunities:

The next choir/dance/music ministry rehearsal is:

My spirit was renewed by:

I will practice what was taught today by:

Date: /   /

Today's sermon was delivered by:	**Today I Feel:**
	☐ Joyous
Today's sermon was about:	☐ Grateful
	☐ Anointed
	☐ In need of prayer
Today's scriptures I plan to study:	☐ Determined
	☐ Like giving God all Praise

I gave this amount to the offering:

This worship song...

This testimony was powerful...

I need to keep   in prayer.

Upcoming Activities of Interest:

Volunteer Opportunities:

The next choir/dance/music ministry rehearsal is:

My spirit was renewed by:

I will practice what was taught today by:

SUNDAY WORSHIP NOTES & REFLECTIONS

Date: /   /

Today's sermon was delivered by:

Today I Feel:
- ☐ Joyous
- ☐ Grateful

Today's sermon was about:

- ☐ Anointed
- ☐ In need of prayer

Today's scriptures I plan to study:

- ☐ Determined
- ☐ Like giving God all Praise

I gave this amount to the offering:

This worship song...

This testimony was powerful...

I need to keep   in prayer.

Upcoming Activities of Interest:

Volunteer Opportunities:

The next choir/dance/music ministry rehearsal is:

My spirit was renewed by:

I will practice what was taught today by:

Kinyatta E. Gray is a Best-Selling Author, Travel Influencer and the CEO of FlightsInStilettos, LLC. Kinyatta is also the Chief Beach Towel Designer for the FlightsInStilettos Glam Girl Beach Towels.

Websites:

https://www.flightsinstilettos.com/

https://www.kinyattagray.com/

https://www.honoringmissbee.com/

Disclaimer:
Kinyatta Gray is not a mental health provider and is providing this information based on her personal experiences. If you are experiencing a mental health crisis, seek the help of a mental health professional.

www.ingramcontent.com/pod-product-compliance
Lightning Source LLC
Chambersburg PA
CBHW070722130626
46553CB00005B/2107